IN MY HEAD

BY

J. M. STORM

Monarch Publishing, 2017
www.monarchbookstore.com

To those who have read and supported my work
over the years, I dedicate this book to you.

1

LIGHTNING FROM A CLEAR BLUE SKY

sometimes you just have
to keep going down
the road of the unknown
and have faith
in the words, not yet
written.

i think some souls
have a way of
connecting without
our knowledge.
that's why you can
meet someone for
the first time,
but inside you just
know. you know it
is not the first
time you've felt
them.

we're all just
a bunch
of addicts,
struggling with
our drug
of choice.

write a list of the things
you would change about them.
then burn it.
because people rarely
change other people.
love changes people
and so does pain.
but mostly, people
change themselves.

one thing i've learned
is that you can lie to
yourself during the day
and get by. but those
lies are worthless
at 2 a.m.
because waking up
in the middle of the
night is when truth
will find you and
there is no escaping it.

i hope that when you
walk down the street,
people see you smile.
and they may wonder
if it is a new love or
maybe a raise at work.
but no, that's not it.
you smile in the knowledge
that everyone you meet
is fighting the same demons
that you are.
you are no better and certainly
no worse. we are all warriors
against a war we fight inside.

one day it happened.
at the train station i set
your baggage down that
i had been carrying for
so long. and i left my ticket
with a note for whomever to
find that read;
i don't belong there,
i never did.
and these aren't
mine to carry,
they never were.

i laughed. i laughed like a kid
when it dawned on me that
so much of what i worried
about wasn't mine to begin
with. what people think
and how they perceive you isn't
in your power.
and yet we let it rob us of who
we truly are.
all in the name of fitting
in with the herd.
and that my friend,
is bullshit.

sometimes you have to leave
because you know there's more.
more that can't be found in
this place and to stay means
to stand still.

one of the surest ways
to hurt yourself is
to have expectations
for someone you
think you know,
but really don't.

some thought she
slipped into madness
for the way she changed.

she thought it was
madness to live the
life she once did.

sometimes you'll feel lost
or that you don't know
where you are going.
be thankful for that.
because that means
you still know what
home feels like, and if
you know what that feels
like, you are never truly lost.

before you pass judgement
on who is self destructing,
it is important to remember
that they usually aren't trying
to destroy themselves.
they are trying to destroy
something inside that
doesn't belong.

the day i changed
was the day i
quit trying to fit
into a world
that never really
fit me.

i know life has us on different
paths, and that is ok.
because that is where
happiness is found,
in the acceptance of reality.
but with that being said,
i sure do hope our
roads cross one more time.

and the deeper you become,
the more some don't know
how to deal with it.
because the deeper you become,
the more truth you reveal.
and truth scares the hell
out of some.
stay deep anyway.

sometimes you are
what they need
and sometimes you
are what they don't
understand, but don't change.
never justify or limit
your madness to keep
someone in your life.

and if she is
in your life,
you must know
she believes you're
a battle worth fighting.

how odd is that
so much of what
isn't said, isn't said
because it is the truth.

maybe life is about
learning a better
goodbye.
learning to let go
of the ones we love
with nothing but love.

life takes a toll
and sometimes she'll
come undone.
she'll unravel and
come apart at the seams.
not because she is weak.
but because she has
been too strong for too long.

you would be surprised as to
what is waiting to walk into
your life, once you learn
to stop running.
because that is what humans do.
we run.
we run from one thing to another.
but once you stop,
you begin to feel more.
you begin to understand.
understanding what is meant to stay
and what is meant to
run away.

and in this life
you'll meet all kinds.
some will want to attach
and some will want
to pull you down.
but there are a few
that you'll meet
that just want to feel
and understand
how your heart made its way
through this world.

2

SOMETHING THAT CUTS LIKE A KNIFE

she didn't just feel,
she felt
indifference.
and that is something
that cuts like a knife
when it comes from someone
you love.
and the truth is that she
just couldn't take anymore scars.

i don't know if a broken heart
really mends or if it just
learns to live in pieces.
we've all had one and
maybe that is by design.
maybe we were never
meant to stay intact.
maybe our beautiful
understanding comes
from our personal
brokenness.

she is a
beautiful piece
of broken
pottery, put
back together by
her own hands.
and a critical world
judges her cracks
while missing the
beauty of how she
made herself
whole again.

she may be falling apart,
but she's been there before.
she'll take her time as
she mourns the pieces
she no longer needs.
and she'll gather the rest
of her, the best of her,
and with a smile,
she'll walk away.

maybe that's all we need.
to know that someone
thinks we're worth the
bad times. to know we're
set apart from the others.
to feel a hand reaching
for us in the dark.

only when you've
felt the blade,
can you truly
understand the scar.

the ones who need
to be held the most
are often too busy
trying to hold others
with their broken arms.

. . .

because sometimes that's what
has to be done. you have to lay
down with it. the hurt. or the
heartache or even the hate.
whatever is inside.
sometimes you have to
get close to it, taste it and
understand it so you can define it,
before it defines you.

. . .

sometimes she'll push away
what she wants because
she wants it too much
and too much scares
the hell out of her.
because sometimes
people lose themselves
in wanting too much.

yeah, I do love
making you laugh
and laugh hard.
because I know
at that very moment,
you are the furthest
away from the things
that hurt you.

sometimes the quietest people
are really screaming inside.

and sometimes the ones with
the deepest understanding of love,
go without it the most.

she was good at convincing
everyone that she was ok.
so good, that she sometimes
believed it as well.

she was far too beautiful
to be so sad. but that is
what we don't realize
so much of the time.
it is easy to look at someone
and think the burdens are light.
it is easy to forget that we all
have a private agony
and we all have a personal hell.

i think there are
so many broken relationships
because there are so many
broken people who won't stop
to heal.

you've made your bed,
now lie in it.
or stand in it.
or burn it to the ground,
i don't care.
it's your bed and
I realized I don't
belong in it.

she gets quiet sometimes
and i can feel a certain weight
has got her by the heart.
and it is in those times
i want her to speak the most,
but i know she can't.
because sometimes things
get grisly inside.
they get messy and she
has to cleanse all that.
and the last thing she wants
to do is dirty me with it.

it takes pain sometimes,
loosen the grip
of that which you were
meant to let go of
a long time ago.

i hope you find
that place one day.
where the chaos
inside is understood
and your heart feels
at home.

i believe your heart
has to be
broken
before you can truly
understand
what it means
to be whole.

3

HOW TO PAINT A MASTERPIECE

she is beautiful
art that tells a story
of losing oneself
and finding it.
you need not know art,
but just listen to her
and feel.
and if you are unable,
you will never understand
she is a masterpiece.

she used to want
a love that she felt
she deserved,
but she's grown
since then.
now she waits for
a love that she
cannot deny.

. . .

and you think you know what
love is, and then someone comes
along and they rewrite
the book. and you realize
that what you knew of love
was so limited and so primitive.
and whether they go or they
happen to remain, one thing is certain.
your life is never really the same.

so many view
love as an option,
when all along
it's been the answer.

even though i know
we would crash,
i would get in the
car with you all
over again.

today i will love you
like there is no tomorrow.

and tomorrow,
i will love you
all over again.

once you get her started,
you had better buckle up.
because she loves full throttle
and that scares the hell
out of some.
those that should have
never handed her the keys.

i am not sure of anything.
but i am certain that
i loved you with a depth
that stars cannot
understand.

4

KISS HER AS THE MOON DOES THE SEA

i've given you
a piece of me.

do something
good with it.

-the universe

she's my kind of beautiful.
that is important to know
because there is beauty
everywhere and yet it
doesn't feel like mine.
but when i saw her,
i wanted to see more.
in the morning when
her hair is a mess and
in the rain when it's
really coming down.
those beautiful everyday moments
that fool her into thinking
she isn't.
I want those.
that's my kind of beautiful.

she sits at the edge
of the ocean, just to think
as she watches the waves break.
she's done that more so
as she's gotten older
and the way life has
thrown so much at her.
because that's the place
where shallow ends
and deep begins.

if you're going to kiss her,
then pull her close and mean it.
kiss her as the moon does the sea.
weightless and yet the deepest
parts of her are moved.

what you have to understand about
her is that she didn't just want
somebody. she wanted somebody
like her, whose roots had never
really settled because they were
waiting to twist with another.

the only flowers
i ever give her
are the wild ones
i pick because
they are the only
that speak to
her genius and
her beauty.
only a wildflower
could ever
understand her.

she loves moonlight
and rainstorms
and so many other
things that have soul.

you are a star
and some skies
aren't big enough
for all that you are.

she's fire
and ice.
you'll fear
the cold and
crave the burn.

one of the things
that she loves most
about the sea
is how it can be both.
both a place to remember
and a place to forget.

you may think she is just
a pretty face, and that is
where you would have it wrong.
she's an olive branch to a man
who has fought too many
wars inside.
she's a green light at a four way
stop because it's been a hell of
a day and you just want to be home.
she's a hornet.
a hurricane,
a masterpiece that my eyes
can't look away from.
you see a pretty face.
i see a soul that is even more so.

part of her mystery
is how she is calm
in the storm
and anxious in
the quiet

if she is your woman,
then you must take
pride in that.
learn her like no one
else has before and
you will know her
like no other, that
i promise.
go ahead. blow her
mind and shatter
her fears.

i fucking dare you.

just be the love of her life.
not the manager of it.
give her love and listen
to her. not for the purpose
to deflect or defend,
but to understand.
it's really that simple.

i don't own her,
no man does.
but there are times
when that's exactly
what she wants
from me.
my hands in
her hair
and owning
all that she is.

she wants to be
controlled sometimes,
but by a man who
knows about control.
and that is revealed
in how well
he is able
to control himself.

a strong woman
needs a strong man
who'll give her
powerful love.
she'll never be
satisfied with the
weak of heart.

yeah, she's a circus.

but soon you'll want
to run away with her
and never come back.

love her harder
than her insecurities.
love her deeper
than her deepest fears
and prove to her
that love conquers all.

she doesn't need
to be held down
or held back.
she just needs
to be held.
and when you
understand her,
you'll understand
exactly what that means.

love her in the morning
when her hair is a mess
and she hasn't had
a chance to put her
makeup on.
because that's a quiet
love that speaks to her
so loudly.

. . .

you look at her
and only see she
is hot,
so ignorant of
all the ways
she can burn you.

in your dark days, just turn
around and i will be there.
and maybe i won't have
any more light to give than
what you already have.
but I will take your hand
and we will find the
light together.

i will not lie to you,
even if the truth
may drive you away.
because if you have to
lie to keep someone,
then they never were
really yours.

don't take her for granted,
even when her walls come down.
she still has her guard up
and that will take some time
for her to work out.
because it is a big world
and a bit scary without walls.

she can take care of
herself just fine.
still she only wants a man
who is willing to lay it all
on the line to make
sure she is ok.
but she will never ask for that.

the truth that
many men never realize
is that how they
view a woman
says more about
themselves
than about her.

she loved him like
no one before him because
of the way he loved her.
it was the way he gave her
freedom and yet when she
needed it, he gave her
the firm grip of control.
and for her, one just wasn't
the same without the other.

and you'll know it is her,
the one, when your life
shifts and the most
important thing to you
is giving her laughter
and moments of paradise.
not because you're expected,
but because any less feels
like a certain hell.

never underestimate
the power of making
her pancakes
on a Sunday morning.

you can skip the act
because she knows
bullshit when she
smells it.
she doesn't want
a fairy tale,
she just wants real.

give him respect
as much as you give
him love.
because that's a big
thing for a man,
to be respected by
the woman he loves.
but you will also
know what kind of man
he is by in the way
he treats that respect.

6

THE MONSTERS HAVE TO FALL ASLEEP

every night she
sings lullabies
to her burdens
and fears
because that's
what has to be
done.
the monsters
have to fall
asleep before
she can.

I know how it feels
to live in a world
that always falls
for the look
while you always
fall for the feel.

the feeling is just the beginning.
you have to learn how to sift
and understand them.
asking yourself why
something makes you sad or
happy or reflective.
and once you understand that,
you'll understand how you work.
what your weaknesses are
and what is your strength.
and that is powerful.
that is unique. that is in control.
and in today's world, that
is a rarity.

you are the book that i never
grow tired of reading and i
bend the corners of my favorite
pages, the involuntary things
you make me do.
the joy i cannot
contain that comes
from somewhere deep
and it erupts into laughter.
the smile that your
spirit always coaxes out
just by being you.
the lump in my throat
when you're sad and
i just want to fix it, but i
know i cant.
things beyond my control,
like heartbeats and breaths.

I know you're scared,
but it is not of me.
you're afraid of the realness.
you're fearful for the first
time in your life of something
you can't walk away from,
and that scares the hell out of you.

the mind remembers
the words, but the heart
remembers how it feels.
the mind can forget,
but the heart never will.

the truth is
i am crazy
about you
and every day
i go a little
more mad.

and i need you.
not in the ways
to survive, but
in the ways that
make life worth
living.

maybe we didn't
know each other
like we believed
and maybe we
never really did.
but I want you
to know that
whatever my mind
made you into,
it was always
beautiful.

she's not ok with
the same old risks
because she no
longer has the
same old heart.
she's grown and
she's healed and
she's become
aware of more.

i am not afraid
to die alone.
i am afraid
of looking
back on my chapters
as a lie.

one of the things
I love most about you
is that you don't
need me for anything.
and yet, you find
yourself needing me.

make someone
smile every day.
but never forget
that you are
someone too.

she was the type of girl
who didn't share much
because sharing meant
digging around in the past.
because for some,
history is too painful
and there are so many
better things to do
than flip through
pages of pain.

this time is going to
be different, she thought.
because this time i have no
expectations beyond today.
and today, feels pretty good.

so many in this world
search for home and yet
many will stay lost.
because they think
too much and feel
too little.
and that is the whisper
in the secret.
home has always
been about how
it feels.

we
remember
the things
that make
us feel.

7

ADDICTED TO THE WILD THINGS

she is beautiful.
but you really cannot
comprehend it until
you understand that
she is the result
of the pieces
that she refused
to let life take from her.

she's a beautiful
question that
the brightest men
can't answer.
but the wisest
man knows she is
impossible to sum
up with an answer
because she is full
of possibility.

i thought of her
heart as a church
that felt sacred
and holy.
i always thought
of her mind as if
she were drinking shots
while reading me
poetry in a low cut dress.

she's a strong
cup of black coffee
in a world that is
drunk on the cheap
wine of shallow love.

she is kind, but strong.
and that is where
so many mistake her.
they interpret her
kindness for weakness
and force her to
show her strength.

she was a true lady
in every sense
of the word.
but make no mistake,
when it came to love,
she was ready
to go bare knuckles.

the parts of you
that will never be tamed
are the parts
i crave the most.
i am addicted
to the wild things
in you.

she is the type
of woman who only
shows you
her bad girl
when she believes
in your good man.

WHERE TO FOLLOW JMSTORM

FACEBOOK: facebook.com/Jmstormquotes

TUMBLR: jmstormquotes.tumblr.com

INSTAGRAM: @jmstormquotes

TWITTER: @storm_jon